Contents

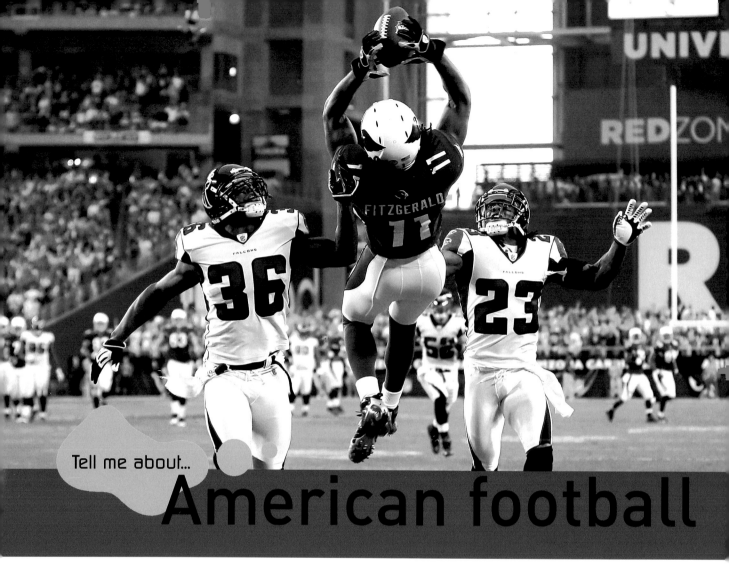

Tell me about...

American football

▲

Larry Fitzgerald takes a spectacular catch to score a touchdown for the Arizona Cardinals in 2009. The Cardinals beat the Atlanta Falcons 30-24.

American football is an all-action team sport. The two teams in a game try to move the ball up the field to score points by kicking a field goal, or by moving the ball into an area of the field called the end zone to score a touchdown. The team with the most points wins!

A complete game of American football is made up of four 15-minute-long quarters. In the professional game, if the scores are level at the end of full time, a 15-minute period of overtime is played. There are many stoppages and teams are allowed short breaks called time-outs, which means that a full game can last three or four hours.

Players can move the ball by running with it, throwing it to a team-mate or kicking it. A team gets four chances, each called a down, to move the ball at least 10 yards (9.1m) forward. If the players succeed, they are given a new set of four downs. This is called getting a first down. If they fail, the ball is handed to the opposing team.

Although only 11 players per team are on the field at one time, an American football team may contain up to 45 players. These are split into offence (players who play when their team has the ball), defence and special teams (see pages 22-23).

Players in defence try to stop the opposition from scoring field goals and touchdowns. They also run and tackle hard to stop them from gaining the distance they need to make the first down.

▲ Thumping tackles are a big feature of American football. Here, Clinton Portis is driven back by two members of the New York Giants team.

▼ The quarterback is the player who makes most of the passes when playing offence. Here, he has spotted that one of his receivers is free and throws a forward pass.

Touchdown!

A receiver is free, the quarterback spots him and sends the ball high. The receiver catches it, avoids a tackle and runs into the end zone. Touchdown! That's the score every team wants to make. It's worth six points.

Despite its name, a touchdown does not mean that the ball has to touch the ground. To score, a player must carry the ball into the end zone or catch it in the end zone.

After a successful touchdown, the team that has scored gets a chance to earn an extra point. The ball is snapped

▼ The Arizona Cardinals' Tim Hightower dives into the end zone to score a touchdown against the Kansas City Chiefs.

▲ Great teamwork has sent this receiver free with the ball to run into the end zone to score a touchdown.

Record-breakers

The biggest competition in American football is the National Football League or NFL. Jerry Rice holds the NFL record for the most touchdowns in a career. He made 208 including a record-tying five as a receiver in a single game!

Atlanta Falcons kicker Morten Anderson holds the record for the most points in NFL history with 2,544.

back (passed back) from the three yard line to a kicker who tries to strike the ball through the two goal posts, called uprights, to score a one point conversion. The team can also gamble on scoring two points by taking the ball from the three-yard line and crossing into the end zone for a second time.

There are two other ways of scoring points. A safety is worth two points. It is scored by defenders tackling opponents with the ball in the opposing team's own end zone. A field goal, worth three points, is scored when, during play,

the players in the offensive team pass the ball to their kicker, who is close enough to attempt to kick the ball through the uprights.

▼ Morten Anderson kicks the conversion for the Atlanta Falcons that made him the all-time leading points scorer in 2006.

Super Bowl stars

The NFL's championship game at the end of each season is called the Super Bowl. Every NFL player hopes to play in it. The NFL regular season starts at the beginning of September and runs through to early February. Before the season starts there are training sessions: the Organized

▼ NFL training camps involve lots of hard work. Here a player practises his blocking using a blocking sled at the Green Bay Packers 2007 training camp.

The Most Valuable Players

Joe Montana has won three Most Valuable Player (MVP) awards in Super Bowl finals, a record number of wins.

In Super Bowl XLII in 2008, the New York Giants quarterback, Eli Manning, was the MVP. The year before, the MVP was awarded to the Indianapolis Colts quarterback – Eli's brother, Peyton!

▲ Eli and Peyton Manning both throw a ball at a special event for NFL fans held in New York City. Top NFL stars are expected to help promote the sport to spectators.

Team Activities take place in the spring and the summer training camp usually begins in July. The regular season consists of the 32 teams playing 16 games. The top twelve teams enter a series of play-off games with the Super Bowl held in February.

Top NFL players are paid well and often wealthy but they must train incredibly hard, work out a lot in the gym and be careful about what they eat. It's a tough, impact sport with lots of contact and many players suffer from injuries.

Summer training allows a new coach and players to become familiar with their team but the pressure is also on. A team may enter the summer training camp with as many as 80 players but must trim its roster (or team list) to a maximum of 53 players before the season starts. Every player is fighting for a place.

Equipment and the field

▲ Players suit up in their team's locker room before the game. Some players wear a neck roll which stops the head being snapped back too far.

American football players often collide with enormous power, so they wear a lot of protective clothing to reduce the chance of injury.

An athletic supporter which protects the groin, and thigh, knee, rib and elbow pads are worn. Helmets come with face masks or visors, a mouth guard and a chin guard.

The most complicated piece of equipment to wear is the set of shoulder pads. These are made up of several pieces and come in different types depending on a player's position. For example, quarterbacks may wear a lighter set of shoulder pads than linebackers who tackle heavily and frequently.

An American football field is 109.7m long and 49m wide. At each end is a 9.1m-deep end zone. At the back of each end zone is a set of uprights. There are lines across the field every 4.6m known as five yard lines. Every second line has a number showing the distance in yards to the nearest end zone.

◄

This player with the ball has run over the sideline and is out of bounds. The game will restart with the next play taken from the nearest hash mark. The player must have control of the ball before going out of bounds.

An American football field

Hash marks every yard (0.91 metres) up the field.

Goal posts (uprights)

50 yard halfway line

Sideline

Goal line

End zone

End line

The line of scrimmage

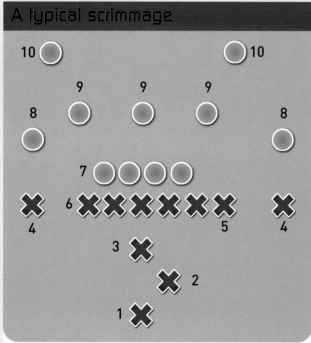

A typical scrimmage

Offence		Defence
1. Running back	4. Wide receiver	7. Defensive line
2. Fullback	5. Tight end	8. Cornerback
3. Quarterback	6. Offensive line	9. Linebacker
		10. Safety

Each down begins with the two teams lining up on either side of the line of scrimmage. This is where the officials rule the ball should be, either for a penalty or because it's where the player with the ball was tackled on the previous down.

The offence can line up in different ways. Usually, this includes a line of big, strong players called offensive linemen. In the middle of these is the centre whose job it is to snap the ball back to the quarterback. Other players on offence may include a tight end, wide receivers, a half-back and a fullback.

A down begins with the centre snapping the ball back to the quarterback. The defensive team aims to get past the offensive linemen and either tackle the quarterback before he passes or

► The 'chain crew' are the officials equipped with a ten-yard chain which they use to measure whether a team has gained enough distance to get a first down.

▲ An offensive lineman has one hand on the ground (a three-point stance). He faces a defensive lineman who is in a four-point stance with both hands on the ground.

tackle the running back with the ball. The offensive linemen try to stop them by blocking (see page 21). Other defenders called cornerbacks and safeties track other opponents such as fast receivers.

If the ball lands out of bounds or touches the ground from a pass before anyone catches it, then the pass is ruled incomplete and the next down begins from the same place as the last. If the ball is caught by a receiver or held by a running back, the next down begins from where that player was tackled or ran out of bounds.

▼ This centre performs a shotgun snap, passing the ball back four or five metres to the quarterback and giving him extra time and space to play.

The quarterback

The quarterback is the team's leader during offence. He receives the coach's instructions and explains the play to his team before the down starts.

▲ Throwing a ball well takes lots of practice. The thrower steps forward, turning his hips and shoulders to face the target. The ball is released with a flick of the wrist to help it spin and travel smoothly towards its target.

The quarterback receives the ball from the centre and usually retreats by taking some steps backwards with his head up. He can then make one of three types of play. He may hand the ball to a running back, run with the ball himself or throw the ball to a receiver. A high, long throw to a receiver heading towards the end zone is called a bomb.

Although a quarterback usually carries out his coach's instructions, he may change the play in the last seconds before the snap. This is called an audible. Quarterbacks expect protection from their team's offensive linemen. If opponents break through and if the quarterback takes too long with his pass, he risks being tackled behind the line of scrimmage. This is called a sack.

▲ This quarterback (middle) is about to hand the ball to a running back who will try to sprint and weave his way through a gap.

▼ This is a good grip with the fingers spread, the little finger on the middle of the laces and the first finger near the back of the ball.

Quarterbacks

Quarterbacks are often the highest paid players on an NFL team. In 2008, Ben Roethlisberger signed a contract with the Pittsburgh Steelers worth 102 million dollars over eight years!

Brett Favre holds many NFL quarterback records including most touchdown passes (454), most passes completed (5,464) and most starts in a row for a quarterback, an amazing 257.

In the NFL, quarterbacks and defensive players have microphones and speakers inside their helmets so that they can be in radio contact with their coach.

Receiving

A completed pass not only needs a good throw from the quarterback but a skilled run and catch from the receiver. Receivers keep their eyes on the ball until it is in their hands. As the ball arrives, they relax their hands to cushion its landing and try to bring it in towards their body to protect it.

Receivers don't want to make a fumble and drop the ball before they are tackled or ruled as down. Neither do they want the passes that are aimed at them to be intercepted, or caught by an opponent. Interceptions can often lead to a touchdown for the other team. This is because the offensive team is not in a good position to defend.

▶

These two young players are enjoying practising their throwing and catching. Catching a football takes lots of practice to develop the skill so it will work when running fast and under pressure from opponents.

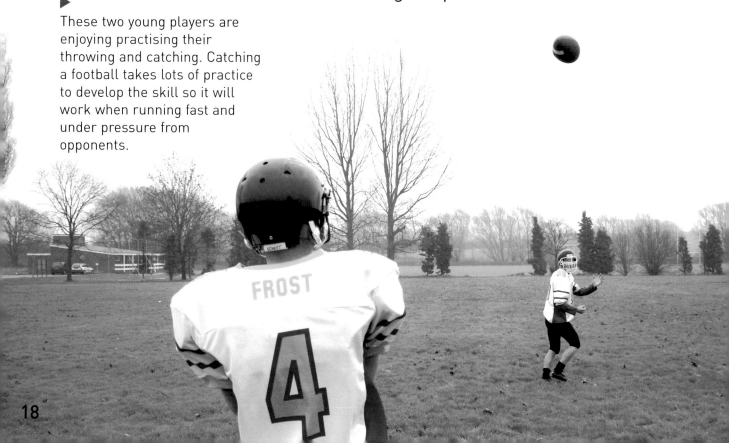

Catching the ball is only part of a receiver's job. Receivers have to use their speed and skill to get away from any opponents defending them to receive the pass. Sometimes, teams use complicated plays to outwit the other team to set a receiver free. Once they have the ball, receivers sprint hard and may use swerves to keep free of defenders to run as far as they can. Receivers must also block on running plays.

Long passes can be risky, so sometimes a team will use their running backs. These players are often handed the ball by the quarterback and try to burst through gaps created by their team-mates blocking and creating space.

▼ This receiver is sprinting hard and in lots of space. He holds the ball one-handed, cradled in between the side of his body and his elbow. His free hand can be used to fend off opponents.

▼ This wide receiver has outsprinted the defence and has leapt high to catch a high pass safely.

Tackling and blocking

Stopping the other team from scoring and gaining a first down is very important for the defending team. Its players try to tackle the player with the ball as quickly as possible before their opponents can gain crucial territory.

Tacklers must time their tackles carefully. They can cause a 'pass interference penalty' if they tackle receivers before they have caught the ball. In the NFL, this means the offensive team moves the ball to where the pass would have been caught.

▼ Tacklers tend to aim for the waist, driving their shoulder into the other player's stomach and wrapping their arms around him to stop him and either drive him out of bounds or stop him from moving forward.

▲ These linemen (in white shirts) are pass blocking, keeping their opponents at bay long enough for their quarterback to make a good pass.

Before the officials signal a down, tacklers are allowed to strip the ball, meaning they wrestle it free of their opponent. This may occur when a second tackler arrives to help.

Blocking is a crucial skill in offence. It is keeping defenders away from a team-mate with the ball. Blocking attempts occur at every scrimmage when the linemen try to keep the opposition defenders away from the quarterback. Blocking can also create gaps for a running back to run through with the ball or or for a receiver to catch the ball.

Blockers can use their hands or arms to push defenders away but must not hold onto them or tackle them. Blocks cannot be made in the back of an opponent or from behind and below the waist, which is called clipping. If either happens, the team will lose yardage.

Special teams

When kicking or returning a kick is needed, it's time to call on special teams. These players may only be on the field for a few moments of each game, but they can make the difference between a win or a loss.

▲ This player makes a long punt. See how high his kicking foot follows through. This helps the ball travel further.

A member of the special teams starts every game by kicking off – kicking the ball deep into opposition territory. A kick-off is also used to restart the game after a team has scored points. Special teams come out for field goal attempts worth three points and for conversions after a touchdown worth one point.

▲
A team-mate holds the ball in position with his fingers. The kicker can take a good length run-up and will aim for a fast, powerful kick.

▲
This punt returner has gathered the ball in safely and is now running forward. He aims to gain as much territory as possible before he is tackled.

Teams often choose to punt when they are on their fourth down and a long way away from gaining a first down. The punter stands around 10 metres or more back from the line of scrimmage. He must catch the ball, step forward and drop kick the ball smoothly and quickly. His team-mates will chase the punt and aim to tackle the opponent with the ball to make the first down as far away from their own end zone as possible.

When one team decides to punt other than at a kick-off, the receiving team will bring on its own special team players. This will include a kick or punt returner who catches the ball and returns it up the field as far as possible.

▼ A field goal needs players to work closely together. The centre snaps the ball back to the holder who catches it and places it in position for the kicker to strike.

Flag football

A player adjusts her belt and holds one of the flags which are attached to the side.

Many players enjoy versions of American football where there is less contact and no need to wear a helmet and lots of padding. One of the most popular is flag football. It is a good way for both boys and girls to get into American football and learn some of the skills of the sport.

Flag footballers wear little or no padding but do wear one or two pieces of material called flags attached to a belt. If an opponent grabs and removes a flag from the player holding the ball, then that player is de-flagged.

When the flag is removed, the down is over. The next down will start from where the flag was removed. Whether you are playing in defence or offence, you will need to be sharp and react quickly to opponents to make or avoid a tackle.

In Britain, most flag football games are played on a field around 50m long and 25m wide and with five players a side. The U.S. Flag Football Association (USFFA) rules play eight players a side on a pitch 80 yards (73m) long. Blocks are allowed between the waist and shoulders but holding is not allowed.

▲ The player with the ball is about to lose her flag. Once it has been removed from the belt, she is tackled and the down is over.

▼ Scrimmages occur in flag football with the aim still being to gain enough distance for a first down.

The world of American football

The NFL may be the peak of American football but there are dozens of other competitions both in North America and around the world. Many of these follow slightly different rules from those of the NFL.

College football played by students is very popular in the United States. Top games sell out 100,000 seat stadiums. Women's football is also played with different national leagues in America including the Independent Women's Football League and the National Women's Football Association.

▼ Miaya Tolbert playing for Detroit Demolition is caught and tackled by two members of the Chicago Force. This Independent Women's Football League game ended with Detroit winning 19-0.

▲ New York Dragons' Chin Achebe scores a touchdown against the Dallas Desperados. This Arena Football League game was played indoors at New York's Nassau Coliseum.

Although the sport's home is in the United States, it is popular elsewhere, too. National leagues in countries include the German Football League, Japan's 60-team X-League and the British American Football League (BAFL). There have been three American Football World Cup competitions as well, with Japan winning the first two and the United States the third one in 2007.

In competition

The very first game the USA played in the 2007 World Cup saw them thrash South Korea 77-0!

The London Olympians are the most successful BritBowl team with 11 appearances in the BritBowl and nine championship titles.

In 1916, a college game between the Cumberland Bulldogs and Georgia Tech Engineers entered the record books. Georgia Tech won by an incredible score...222-0!

Where next?

These websites and books will help you to find out more about American football.

http://www.nfluk.com   http://www.nflrush.com
This website includes brief guides to all 32 NFL teams and a searchable map of the UK showing which British teams are closest to you. NFL Rush is a great children's companion website to the main NFL website. It contains videos of game action, star players and lots of fun activities.

http://www.sikids.com/
The famous *Sports Illustrated* magazine has a special website for younger fans. It contains lots of fun games as news, results and other features on both NFL and NCCA football.

http://www.bafl.org.uk/
The website of the British American Football League contains links and results of all British league teams as well as youth and flag football teams.

http://www. Londonblitz.com/
The website of the London Blitz American Football team contains lots of links to both other British websites and the websites of the NFL and its teams.

There is no single overall organisation in charge of flag football. So, organise a search of the internet with an adult to find out all about flag football in your country or region.

http://www.talkamericanfootball.co.uk/
A really useful news and blog site with good guides to playing positions and the sport's history as well as a good selection of UK links in its Getting Started section.

Books
Football: A History of the Gridiron Game - Mark Stewart (Childrens Press 1999).
Everything Kids' Football Book - Greg Jacobs (Adams Media, 2008).
Football Skills: How to Play Like a Pro - Martin Gitlin (Elmslow Elementary, 2008).

American football words

audible a change of move call usually made by a quarterback to his team-mates

blocking when players on offense try to stop opponents from reaching the ball carrier using their hands and body

down a play in American football, starting with the pass made by a centre and ending when the officials rule the play is over

field goal a kick through the goal uprights worth three points

intercepted when a throw by one team is caught by a player from the other team

penalty a punishment given out by the officials to a team who breaks the rules during a game

punt a high kick, made by dropping the ball from the hands, which is designed to drive the other team back as far as possible

sack when the quarterback is tackled behind where the ball started on a down

snapped the way a centre starts play in a down by passing or handing the ball to a team-mate

special teams players who come on the field when the ball is to be punted or kicked

strip to remove the ball from an opponent during a tackle

time-outs a break in play which can be called by either team or the officials

touchdown running or catching the ball in the end zone

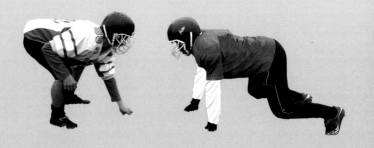

Index

Numbers in **bold** refer to pictures.